HANDS ACROSS THE SEA

Adult
Play File
Coward

A Light Comedy in One Act

by
NOEL COWARD

From

TONIGHT AT 8:30

D1369960

SAMUEL FRENCH

PRINTED IN THE UNITED STATES OF AMERICA

Press and bindery of The Conway Printing Co.
New York

HANDS ACROSS THE SEA

First produced at the Opera House, Manchester, and subsequently at the Phœnix Theatre, Charing Cross Road, London, W.C.2, in January, 1936, with the following cast of characters :

LADY MAUREEN GILPIN (PIGGIE) . .	*Gertrude Lawrence.*
COMMANDER PETER GILPIN, R.N. (her Husband)	*Noel Coward.*
THE HON. CLARE WEDDERBURN . .	*Everley Gregg.*
LIEUT.-COMMANDER ALASTAIR COR-BETT, R.N.	*Edward Underdown.*
MAJOR GOSLING (BOGEY) . . .	*Anthony Pelissier.*
MR. WADHURST	*Alan Webb.*
MRS. WADHURST	*Alison Leggatt.*
MR. BURNHAM	*Kenneth Carten.*
WALTERS	*Moya Nugent.*

The action of the play takes place in the drawing-room of the Gilpins' flat in London.

TIME.—Present day.

HANDS ACROSS THE SEA

Produced by John C. Wilson at the National Theatre in New York City on November 24, 1936, as one of a series of nine one-act plays by Noel Coward, under the title of "TO-NIGHT AT EIGHT-THIRTY." The play was directed by the author and the cast was as follows:

LADY MAUREEN GILPIN (PIGGIE) .	*Gertrude Lawrence.*
COM. PETER GILPIN, R.N. . . .	*Noel Coward.*
LIEUT. COM. ALASTAIR CORBETT, R.N.	*Edward Underdown.*
MRS. WADHURST	*Joyce Carey.*
MR. WADHURST	*Alan Webb.*
MR. BURNHAM	*Kenneth Carten.*
THE HON. CLARE WEDDERBURN . .	*Joan Swinstead.*
MAJOR GOSLING (BOGEY) . .	*Anthony Pelissier.*
WALTERS	*Moya Nugent.*

The action of the play takes place in the drawing-room of the Gilpins' flat in London.

TIME.—Present Day.

HANDS ACROSS THE SEA

The Scene *is the drawing-room of the* Gilpins' *f t in London. The time is about 6 p.m. The room is nicely furnished and rather untidy.*

When the Curtain *rises the telephone is ringing.* Walters, *a neat parlourmaid, enters* R., *and answers it.*

Walters (*at the telephone*). Hallo . . . Yes . . . No, her ladyship's not back yet . . . She said she'd be in at five, so she ought to be here at any minute now . . . What name, please . . . Rawlingson . . . Mr. and Mrs. Rawlingson . . . (*She scribbles on the pad.*) Yes . . . I'll tell her . . .

(*She hangs up the receiver and goes out* R. *There is the sound of voices in the hall and* Lady Maureen Gilpin *enters, followed at a more leisurely pace by her husband,* Peter Gilpin. Maureen, *nicknamed* Piggie *by her intimates, is a smart, attractive woman in the thirties.* Peter *is tall and sunburned and reeks of the Navy.*)

Piggie (*as she comes in*). . . . and you can send the car back for me at eleven-thirty. It's quite simple, darling. I wish you wouldn't be so awfully complicated about everything.

Peter. What happens if my damned dinner goes on longer than that and I get stuck ?

Piggie (*puts her hat on the telephone table*). You just get stuck, darling, and then you get unstuck and get a taxi——

Peter (*grumbling*). I shall be in uniform, clinking with medals——

Piggie. If you take my advice you'll faint dead

7

away at eleven o'clock and then you can come home in the car and change and have time for everything——

PETER (*gets a cigarette from the cocktail table*). I can't faint dead away under the nose of the C.-in-C.

PIGGIE. You can feel a little poorly, can't you ? Anybody has the right to feel a little poorly—— (*She sees the telephone-pad.*) My God !

PETER. What is it ?

PIGGIE. The Rawlingsons.

PETER. Who the hell are they ? (*He crosses* C.)

PIGGIE. I'd forgotten all about them—I must get Maud at once—— (*She sits on the back upstage end of the sofa and dials a number.*)

PETER. Who are the Rawlingsons ?

PIGGIE. Maud and I stayed with them in Samolo, I told you about it, that time when we had to make a forced landing—they practically saved our lives—— (*At the telephone.*) Hullo—Maud—darling, the Rawlingsons are on us . . . What . . . the RAWLINGSONS —yes—I asked them to-day and forgot all about it . . . You must come at once . . . But, darling, you *must* . . . Oh, dear . . . No no, that was the Frobishers ; these are the ones we stayed with.

(PETER *sits in the armchair* R.C.)

Mother and father and daughter—you must remember —pretty girl with bad legs . . . No . . . They didn't have a son . . . We swore we'd give them a lovely time when they came home on leave . . . I know they didn't have a son, that was those other people in Penang . . . Oh, all right . . . You'll have to do something about them, though . . . Let me ask them to lunch with you to-morrow . . . All right . . . one-thirty . . . I'll tell them . . . (*She hangs up.*) She can't come. (*She goes down* L.)

PETER. You might have warned me that a lot of Colonial strangers were coming trumpeting into the house——

PIGGIE. I tell you I'd forgotten——

PETER. That world trip was a grave mistake——

PIGGIE. Who can I get that's celebrated (*she crosses* R.)—to give them a thrill ?

PETER. Why do they have to have a thrill ?

PIGGIE (*runs over to the telephone*). I'll get Clare, anyway—— (*She dials another number.*)

PETER. She'll frighten them to death.

PIGGIE. Couldn't you change early and come in in your uniform ? That would be better than nothing——

PETER. Perhaps they'd like to watch me having my bath !

PIGGIE (*at the telephone*). I want to speak to Mrs. Wedderburn, please . . . Yes . . . (*To* PETER.) I do wish you'd be a little helpful——

PETER. I wish you wouldn't attack me.

PIGGIE (*at the telephone*). Clare ? . . . This is Piggie . . . I want you to come round at once and help me with the Rawlingsons . . . No, I know you haven't, but that doesn't matter . . . Mother, father and daughter—very sweet—I'm repaying hospitality . . . Maud's having them to lunch to-morrow and Peter's going to take them over the Dockyard . . .

PETER (*jumps up*). I'm not going to do any such thing——

PIGGIE. Shut up. I just thought of that and it's a *very* good idea—— (*At the telephone.*) All right, darling—as soon as you can . . . (*She hangs up.*) I must go and change—— (*She picks up her hat.*)

PETER. You know perfectly well I haven't time to take mothers and fathers and daughters with bad legs over the dockyard——

PIGGIE. It wouldn't take a minute ; they took us all over their rubber plantations. (*She crosses to* PETER *above the sofa.*)

PETER. It probably served you right.

PIGGIE. You're so disobliging, darling ; you really should try to conquer it. It's something to do with being English, I think—as a race I'm ashamed of us —no sense of hospitality. The least we can do when people are kind to us in far-off places is to be a little gracious in return.

PETER.   They weren't kind to me in far-off places.

PIGGIE.   You know there's a certain grudging, sullen streak in your character—I've been very worried about it lately—it's spreading like a forest fire——

PETER.   Why don't you have them down for the week-end ?

PIGGIE.   Don't be so idiotic, how can I possibly ? There's no room to start with, and even if there were they'd be utterly wretched——

PETER.   I don't see why.

PIGGIE.   They wouldn't know anybody—they probably wouldn't have the right clothes—they'd keep on huddling about in uneasy little groups——   (*She lights a cigarette from the box on the telephone table.*)

PETER.   The amount of groups that three people can huddle about in is negligible.

(ALASTAIR CORBETT *saunters into the room from* R. *He is good looking and also distinctly naval in tone.*)

ALLY.   Hallo, chaps.

PIGGIE.   Ally darling—how lovely—we're in trouble. Peter'll tell you all about it——

(*The telephone rings and she goes to it. The following conversations occur simultaneously.*)

ALLY.   What trouble ?

PETER.   More of Piggie's beach friends.

ALLY.   Let's have a drink.

PETER.   Cocktail ?

ALLY.   No, a long one—whisky and soda.

PETER (*going to the drink table*).   All right.

ALLY.   What beach friends ?

PETER.   People Maud and Piggie picked up in the East.

PIGGIE (*at the telephone*).   Hulloh . . .   Yes—Robert dear—how lovely ! . . .   It's Robert . . .

ALLY.   Piggie ought to stay at home more.

(PETER *mixes a whisky and soda.*)

PIGGIE (*on the telephone*).   Where are you ?

PETER. That's what I say!

PIGGIE. Oh, what a shame . . . No—Peter's going to sea on Thursday—I'm going down on Saturday.

ALLY. Rubber, I expect. Everybody in the East's rubber.

PIGGIE (*on the telephone*). No—nobody particular —just Clare and Bogey, and I think Pops, but he thinks he's got an ulcer or something and might not be able to come!

PETER. We thought you might be a real friend and take them over the dockyard.

ALLY. What on earth for?

PETER. Give them a thrill.

PIGGIE (*on the telephone*). All right—I'll expect you . . . No, I don't think it can be a very big one —he looks as bright as a button.

ALLY. Why don't you take them over the dockyard?

PETER. I shall be at sea Thursday—exercises!

PIGGIE (*on the telephone*). No, darling, what is the use of having her—she only depresses you . . . Oh, all right! (*She hangs up.*) Oh dear——

PETER. It's quite easy for you—you can give them lunch on board——

ALLY. We're in dry dock.

PETER. They won't mind. What is it?

PIGGIE. Robert—plunged in gloom—he's got to do a course at Greenwich—he ran into a tram in Devonport—and he's had a row with Molly. He wants me to have her for the week-end so that they can make it up all over everybody. Have you told Ally about the Rawlingsons?

PETER. Yes, he's taking them over the Dockyard, lunching them on board and then he's going to show them a submarine——

PIGGIE. Marvellous. You're an angel, Ally. I must take off these clothes, I'm going mad——

(*She goes out of the room up* L.C. *at a run. There is the sound of the front-door bell.*)

✸✸

PETER. Let's go into my room—I can show you the plans——

ALLY. Already? They've been pretty quick with them.

PETER. I made a few alterations—there wasn't enough deck space. She ought to be ready by October. I shall have her sent straight out to Malta——

ALLY. Come on, we shall be caught——

(*They go off up* L.C. *as* WALTERS *ushers in* MR. *and* MRS. WADHURST *on the* R. *The* WADHURSTS *are pleasant, middle-aged people; their manner is a trifle timorous.*)

WALTERS. Her ladyship is changing; I'll tell her you are here.

MRS. WADHURST. Thank you.

MR. WADHURST. Thank you very much.

(WALTER *goes out up* L.C. *The* WADHURSTS *look round the room,* C.)

MRS. WADHURST. It's a very nice flat.

MR. WADHURST. Yes—yes, it is.

MRS. WADHURST (*crosses* L., *scrutinizing a photograph on the piano*). That must be him.

MR. WADHURST. Who?

MRS. WADHURST. The Commander.

(WALTERS *enters up* L.C., *crosses and exits* R.)

MR. WADHURST. Yes—I expect it is.

MRS. WADHURST. Sailors always have such nice open faces, don't they?

MR. WADHURST. Yes, I suppose so.

MRS. WADHURST (*comes* C.). Clean-cut and look-you-straight-in-the-eye—I like men who look you straight in the eye. (*She crosses up* R.)

MR. WADHURST. Yes, it's very nice. (*He follows her.*)

MRS. WADHURST (*at another photograph on the half-moon table up* R.). This must be her sister—I recognize her from " The Tatler "—look. She was Lady Hurstley, you know, then she was Lady Macfadden, and I don't know who she is now.

MR. WADHURST. Neither do I. (*His back to the audience.*)

MRS. WADHURST. What a dear little boy—such a sturdy little fellow—look at the way he's holding his engine.

MR. WADHURST. Is that his engine?

MRS. WADHURST. He has rather a look of Donald Hotchkiss, don't you think?

MR. WADHURST. Yes, dear.

MRS. WADHURST. I must say they have very nice things—— Oh, dear, how lovely to be well off—— I must write to the Brostows by the next mail and tell them all about it.

MR. WADHURST. Yes, you must.

MRS. WADHURST. Don't you think we'd better sit down?

MR. WADHURST. Why not?

MRS. WADHURST. You sit in that chair and I'll sit on the sofa.

MR. WADHURST. Yes, dear.

(*She sits on the sofa. He sits in the armchair.*)

MRS. WADHURST. I wish you wouldn't look quite so uncomfortable, Fred, there's nothing to be uncomfortable about.

(*He puts his elbow on the arm of the chair.*)

MR. WADHURST. She does expect us, doesn't she?

MRS. WADHURST. Oh yes, I talked to her myself on the telephone last Wednesday; she was perfectly charming and said that we were to come without fail and that it would be divine.

MR. WADHURST. I still feel we should have telephoned again just to remind her. People are always awfully busy in London.

MRS. WADHURST. I do hope Lady Dalborough will be here too—I should like to see her again—she was so nice.

MR. WADHURST. She was the other one, wasn't she?

Mrs. Wadhurst (*irritably*). What do you mean, the other one ?

Mr. Wadhurst. I mean not this one.

Mrs. Wadhurst. She's the niece of the Duke of Frensham, her mother was Lady Merrit, she was a great traveller too—I believe she went right across the Sahara dressed as an Arab. In those days that was a very dangerous thing to do.

Mr. Wadhurst. I shouldn't think it was any too safe now.

(Walters *enters* r., *and ushers in* Mr. Burnham, *a nondescript young man, carrying a longish roll of cardboard.*)

Walters. The Commander will be here in a minute.

Mr. Burnham. Thanks—thanks very much.

(Walters *goes out.* Mr. Wadhurst *rises.*)

Mrs. Wadhurst (*after a slightly awkward silence*). How do you do.

Mr. Burnham. How do you do.

Mrs. Wadhurst (*with poise*). This is my husband.

Mr. Burnham. How do you do.

Mr. Wadhurst. How do you do.

(*They shake hands.*)

Mrs. Wadhurst (*vivaciously*). Isn't this a charming room ?—so—so lived in.

Mr. Burnham. Yes.

Mr. Wadhurst. Are you in the Navy too ?

Mr. Burnham. No.

Mrs. Wadhurst (*perservering*). It's so nice to be home again—we come from Malaya, you know.

Mr. Burnham. Oh—Malaya.

Mrs. Wadhurst. Yes, Lady Maureen and Lady Dalborough visited us there—my husband has a rubber plantation up country—there's been a terrible slump, of course, but we're trying to keep our heads above water—aren't we, Fred ?

Mr. Wadhurst. Yes, dear, we certainly are.

MRS. WADHURST. Have you ever been to the East ?

MR. BURNHAM. No.

MRS. WADHURST. It's very interesting really, although the climate's rather trying until you get used to it, and of course the one thing we do miss is the theatre——

MR. BURNHAM. Yes—of course.

MRS. WADHURST. There's nothing my husband and I enjoy so much as a good play, is there, Fred ?

MR. WADHURST. Nothing.

MRS. WADHURST. And all we get is films, and they're generally pretty old by the time they come out to us—— (*She laughs gaily.*)

MR. WADHURST. Do you go to the theatre much ?

MR. BURNHAM. No.

(*There is a silence, which is broken by the telephone ringing. Everybody jumps.*)

MRS. WADHURST. Oh, dear—do you think we ought to answer it ?

MR. WADHURST. I don't know.

(*The telephone continues to ring.* CLARE WEDDERBURN *comes in* R. *She is middle aged, well dressed and rather gruff. She is followed by "* BOGEY *"* GOSLING, *a Major in the Marines, a good-looking man in the thirties. He mixes cocktails.*)

CLARE. Hallo—where's the old girl ?

MRS. WADHURST (*nervously*). I—er—I'm afraid I——

(CLARE *crosses and puts her gloves on the piano.* MR. BURNHAM *crosses* L. *and sits on the chair below the piano.*)

CLARE (*going to the telephone*). Mix a cocktail, Bogey —I'm a stretcher case—— (*At the telephone.*) Hallo— no, it's me—Clare . . . God knows, dear . . . Shall I tell her to call you back . . . All right . . . No, it was bloody, darling—a gloomy dinner at the Embassy, then the worst play I've ever sat through, and then the Café de Paris and that awful man who does things with a duck . . . I've already seen him six times, darling . . . Oh, you know, he pinches its behind and it quacks "Land of Hope and Glory" . . . I don't know whether it hurts it or not—I minded at first, but I'm past caring now; after all, it's not like performing dogs; I mind about performing dogs terribly . . . All right . . . Good-bye . . . (*She hangs up and turns to* MRS. WADHURST.) Ducks are pretty bloody, anyway, don't you think? (*She takes a cigarette from her case.*)

MRS. WADHURST. I don't know very much about them.

CLARE. The man swears it's genuine talent, but I think it's the little nip that does it.

MRS. WADHURST. It sounds rather cruel.

CLARE. It's a gloomy form of entertainment, anyhow, particularly as I've always hated "Land of Hope and Glory——"

BOGEY. Cocktail? (*Bringing one for* CLARE *and* MRS. WADHURST.)

CLARE. Thank God!

(BOGEY *hands round cocktails. The* WADHURSTS *and* MR. BURNHAM *accept them and sip them in silence.*)

BOGEY (*going back to the cocktail table*). I suppose Piggie's in the bath.

CLARE. Go and rout her out. (*She takes off her hat and puts it on the piano.*)

BOGEY. Wait till I've had a drink.

CLARE (*to* MRS. WADHURST). Is Peter home or is he still darting about the Solent?

MRS. WADHURST. I'm afraid I couldn't say. You see——

BOGEY. I saw him last night with Janet——

CLARE. Hasn't she had her baby yet?

BOGEY. She hadn't last night.

CLARE. That damned baby's been hanging over us all for months——

(*The telephone rings—*CLARE *answers it.*)

(*Sitting on the telephone table.*) Hallo—yes—hallo, dar-

ling . . . No, it's Clare . . . Yes, he's here . . .
No, I really couldn't face it . . . Yes, if I were likely
to go to India I'd come, but I'm not likely to go to
India . . . I think Rajahs bumble up a house-party
so terribly . . . Yes, I know *he's* different, but the other
one's awful . . . Angela had an agonizing time with
him—all the dining-room chairs had to be changed
because they were leather and his religion prevented
him sitting on them—all the dogs had to be kept out
of the house because they were unclean, which God
knows was true of the Bedlington, but the other ones
were clean as whistles—and then to round everything
off he took Laura Merstham in his car and made passes
at her all the way to Newmarket . . . All right,
darling, here he is . . . (*To* BOGEY.) It's Nina, she
wants to talk to you——

(*She hands the telephone to* BOGEY, *who reaches for it and
lifts the wire so that it just misses* MRS. WADHURST'S
*hat. It isn't quite long enough, so he has to bend down
to speak with his face practically touching her.*)

BOGEY. Excuse me. (*At the telephone.*) Hallo,
Nin . . . I can't on Wednesday. I've got a Guest
Night . . . It's a hell of a long way, it'd take hours
. . .

(CLARE *crosses to the stool by the cocktail table and sits.*
PIGGIE *comes in* L.C. *with a rush.*)

PIGGIE. I am so sorry—— (*She comes below the
sofa and up* C.)
CLARE. Shhh!
BOGEY. Shut up, I can't hear . . .
PIGGIE (*in a shrill whisper*). Who is it?

(PIGGIE *shakes hands with* MRS. WADHURST—*at the top
of the sofa.*)

CLARE. Nina.
BOGEY (*at the telephone*). Well, you can tell George
to leave it for me—and I can pick it up . . .
PIGGIE. How lovely to see you again.

BOGEY. No—I shan't be leaving till about ten—so
if he leaves it by nine-thirty—I'll get it all right . . .

PIGGIE. My husband will be here in a minute—he
has to go to sea on Thursday, but he's arranged for you
to be taken over the Dockyard at Portsmouth——

BOGEY. Give the old boy a crack on the jaw . . .

PIGGIE. It's the most thrilling thing in the world—
You see how the torpedoes are made !—millions of little
wheels inside, all clicking away like mad—and they cost
thousands of pounds each——

BOGEY. No—I saw her last night . . . Not yet,
but at any moment now—I should think . . . All
right—call me at Chatham . . . If I can get away I
shall have to bring Mickie too——

PIGGIE. How much do torpedoes cost——

CLARE. God knows, darling—something fantastic—
ask Bogey——

PIGGIE. Bogey——

BOGEY. What ?

PIGGIE. How much do torpedoes cost each ?

BOGEY. What ? . . . (*At the telephone.*) . . . wait
a minute, Piggie's yelling at me . . .

PIGGIE. Torpedoes—— (*She makes a descriptive
gesture.*)

BOGEY. Oh, thousands and thousands—terribly ex-
pensive things—ask Peter—— (*At the telephone.*) . . .
If I do bring him you'll have to be frightfully nice to
him, he's been on the verge of suicide for weeks . . .

(PIGGIE *reaches for the cigarette-box over the sofa and
offers them to* MRS. WADHURST *and* MR. WADHURST.)

PIGGIE. Don't let her go, I must talk to her——

BOGEY (*at the telephone*). Hold on a minute, Piggie
wants to talk to you . . . All right—I'll let you know
. . . Here she is . . .

(PIGGIE *leans over the sofa and takes the telephone from*
BOGEY, *who steps over the wire and stumbles over*
MRS. WADHURST.)

I'm most awfully sorry——

MRS. WADHURST. Not at all——

PIGGIE (*to* MRS. WADHURST, *sitting at the lower end of the sofa*). It's so lovely you being in England—— (*At the telephone.*) ... Darling—what was the meaning of that sinister little invitation you sent me ?

BOGEY. You know what Mickey is.

PIGGIE. No, dear, I really can't ... I always get so agitated.

CLARE. Well, why does he go on like that ? It's so tiresome.

PIGGIE. I'll come if Clare will ... (*To* CLARE.) Are you going to Nina's Indian ding-dong ?

CLARE. Not without an anæsthetic. (*She puts her bag on the floor.*)

PIGGIE (*at the telephone*). She's moaning a bit, but I'll persuade her ... What happens after dinner ? ... The man with the duck from the Café de Paris ... (*To the room in general.*) She's got that sweet duck from the Café de Paris——

CLARE. Give me another cocktail, Bogey, I want to get so drunk that I just can't hear any more——

PIGGIE (*at the telephone*). But, darling, do you think it's quite *wise* ... I mean, Maharajahs are terribly touchy and there's probably something in their religion about ducks being mortal sin or something ... You know how difficult they are about cows and pigs ... Just a minute ... (*To the* WADHURSTS.) *You* can tell us, of course—— (*She points to* MR. WADHURST *with the 'phone.*)

MR. WADHURST. I beg your pardon.

PIGGIE. Do Indians mind ducks ?

MR. WADHURST. I—I don't think so——

BOGEY. Do you come from India ?

MRS. WADHURST. No, Malaya.

PIGGIE. It's the same sort of thing, though, isn't it— if they don't mind them in Malaya it's *unlikely* that they'd mind them in India—— (*At the telephone.*) ... It'll probably be all right, but you'd better get Douglas Byng as a standby.

CLARE. There might be something in their religion about Douglas Byng. (*She eats an olive.*)

PIGGIE. Everyone's making such a noise. The room's filled with the most dreadful people. (*Looking at* MR. BURNHAM.) Darling, it is definitely Waterloo Station. (*At the telephone.*) No, I'm almost sure he can't—he's going to sea on Thursday . . . Don't be silly, dear, you can't be in the Navy without going to sea *sometimes* . . .

(PETER *enters, up* L.C., *followed by* ALLY.)

(*At the telephone.*) Here he is now, you can ask him yourself . . . (*To* PETER.) Peter, it's Nina, she wants to talk to you—— (*To the* WADHURSTS.) This is my husband and Lieutenant-Commander Corbett—he's been longing to meet you and thank you for being so sweet to us—I told him all about your heavenly house and the plantation—— (*She is up* C.)

MRS. WADHURST (*bridling—to* ALLY). It was most delightful, I assure you, to have Lady Maureen with us——

PIGGIE. Not him, him—that's the wrong one——

MRS. WADHURST. Oh, I'm so sorry——

PETER (*shaking hands with* MRS. WADHURST). It was so kind of you—my wife has talked of nothing else——

PIGGIE (*grabbing him*). Here—Nina's yelling like a banshee—— (*She crosses* R. *for the cigarette-box on the cocktail table and then moves up* C.)

PETER. Excuse me. (*He takes the telephone.*) Hallo, Nin . . . What for ? . . . No, I can't, but Piggie probably can . . . (*To* PIGGIE.) Can you go to Nina's party for the Rajahs ?

PIGGIE. We've been through all that—— (*She offers the cigarettes to the* WADHURSTS.)

PETER. All right—I didn't know—— (*At the telephone.*) . . . No, I shall be at sea for about three days —it isn't tiresome at all, I like it . . .

PIGGIE (*to* MRS. WADHURST). How's your daughter ? (*She fails to light* MR. WADHURST'S *cigarette.*)

MRS. WADHURST (*surprised*). She's a little better, thank you.

PIGGIE. Oh, has she been ill ? I'm so sorry.

MR. WADHURST (*gently*). She's been ill for five years.

PIGGIE (*puzzled*). How dreadful for you—are you happy with that cocktail, or would you rather have tea ? (*She pushes* MR. WADHURST *into the armchair, and sits on the pouffe herself.*)

MRS. WADHURST. This is delicious, thank you. (*She picks up her cocktail and takes a sip.*)

PETER (*at the telephone*). . . . I honestly can't do anything about that, Nina—you might be able to find out from the Admiral . . . Well, if his mother was mad too, that is an extenuating circumstance . . . He'll probably be sent home . . . (*To* CLARE.) Did you know that Freda Bathurst had once been in an asylum ?

CLARE. No, but it explains a lot.

PIGGIE. Why ?

PETER. Her son went mad in Hong-Kong.

CLARE. What did he do ?

PETER. I don't know, but Nina's in a state about it.

PIGGIE. I don't see what it's got to do with Nina——

PETER. He's a relation of some sort——

PIGGIE. See what he did. (*She rises.*)

PETER (*at the telephone*). What did he do, Nina ? . . . Oh . . . Oh, I see . . . Oh . . . Well, he'll certainly be sent home, and a good job too—we can't have that sort of thing in the Service . . . If I were you I'd keep well out of it . . . All right . . . Good-bye. (*He hangs up.*)

PIGGIE. What was it ? (*She sits on the top arm of the sofa.*)

PETER. I couldn't possibly tell you. (*He takes a cigarette from the box on the telephone table.*)

PIGGIE. Poor boy, I expect the climate had something to do with it—the climate's awful in Hong-Kong—look at poor old Wally Smythe——

ALLY (*to the* WADHURSTS). Did you ever know Wally Smythe ?

MRS. WADHURST. No, I'm afraid not.

CLARE. You didn't miss much.

PIGGIE. I adored Wally, he was a darling.

CLARE. He kept on having fights all the time—I do hate people hitting people—— (*To* MRS. WADHURST.) Don't you ?

MRS. WADHURST. Yes.

(*There is suddenly a complete silence.* PIGGIE *breaks it with an effort.*)

PIGGIE (*vivaciously to the* WADHURSTS). Maud was so frightfully sorry that she couldn't come to-day— she's pining to see you again and she asked me to ask you if you'd lunch there to-morrow ?

MRS. WADHURST. How very kind of her.

PIGGIE. She's got a divine little house hidden away in a mews, it's frightfully difficult to find——

(*The telephone rings.* PETER *picks up the telephone and hands it to* PIGGIE.)

I've got millions of questions I want to ask you, what happened to that darling old native who did a dance with a sword ? (*At the telephone.*) Hallo . . . (*Continuing to everyone in general.*) It was the most exciting thing I've ever seen, all the villagers sat round in torch-light and beat——

(MR. BURNHAM *rises and tries to give* PETER *the plans, but he turns his back on them.*)

(*At the telephone.*) Hallo . . . Yes, speaking . . . (*Continuing.*) —beat drums and the—— (*At the telephone.*) Hallo . . . Darling, I'd no idea you were back—(*to everybody*) and the old man tore himself to shreds in the middle, it was marvellous—— (*At the telephone.*) I can't believe it. Where are you speaking from ? . . . My dear, you're *not* ! . . . (*To everybody.*) It's Boodie, she got back last night and she's staying with Norman——

CLARE. Is Phyllis there ?

(PETER *crosses* C.)

PIGGIE (*at the telephone*). Hallo, darling, is Phyllis there ? . . . She's away ? . . . (*To* CLARE.) She's away.

PETER (*to* MR. WADHURST). That's the best joke I ever heard.

CLARE. It's made my entire season, that's all—it's just made it.

(PETER *goes* R. *and talks to* CLARE *and* BOGEY.)

PIGGIE (*at the telephone*). You'd better come and dine to-night . . . I'm on a diet, so there's only spinach, but we can talk . . . Yes, she's here—absolutely worn out—we all are . . . Oh yes, it was pretty grim; it started all right and everything was going beautifully when Vera arrived, unasked, my dear, and more determined than Hitler . . . Of course there was the most awful scene—Alice flounced upstairs with tears cascading down her face and locked herself in the cook's bedroom . . . Clare tried to save the situation by dragging Lady Borrowdale on to the terrace . . .

CLARE (*sibilantly*). *That* was *afterwards* !—— (*She rises and crosses* C.)

PIGGIE (*at the telephone*). Anyhow, hell broke loose . . . You can imagine . . . Janet was there, of course, and we were all worried about her . . . No, it hasn't arrived yet, but the odds are mounting . . . (*To everybody.*) She hasn't had it yet, has she, Peter ?

PETER. If she has, it was born in the gramophone department at Harrods'—I left her there at four-thirty—— (*Crosses* R.)

PIGGIE (*at the telephone*). . . . No, it's still what's known as on the way . . . I'll expect you about eight-thirty . . . I've got to do my feet and then I'm going to relax . . . All right . . . Yes, she's here . . . (*To* CLARE.) Here, Clare, she wants to talk to you—— (*She crosses* R. *a second, then up* C.)

(CLARE, *in order to reach the telephone comfortably, has to kneel on the sofa.*)

CLARE. Excuse me.

MRS. WADHURST. I'm so sorry.

CLARE (*at the telephone*). Darling—I'm dead with surprise . . .

PIGGIE (*to* MRS. WADHURST). Now you must tell me some more——

MRS. WADHURST. Well, really, I don't——

CLARE. Shhhh! I can't hear a word—— (*At the telephone.*) He what? . . . When? . . . He must be raving . . .

PIGGIE (*in a harsh whisper*). Have you still got that sweet dog? (*She sits on the pouffe.*)

MRS. WADHURST (*also whispering*). Yes, we've still got Rudolph.

PIGGIE (*to everybody*). Rudolph's an angel, I can never tell you how divine he was—he used to come in every morning with my breakfast-tray and jump on to the bed——

MRS. WADHURST (*horrified*). Oh, you never told me that. How very naughty of him. He's very seldom allowed in the house at all——

PIGGIE (*puzzled*). But—but——

MR. WADHURST. Perhaps you're thinking of some other dog, Lady Maureen—Rudolph is a Great Dane——

(*They laugh.*)

PIGGIE (*bewildered*). Oh, yes, of course, how idiotic of me——

CLARE (*at the telephone*). . . . All right, darling . . . Call me in the morning . . . Lovely . . . Good-bye. (*She hangs up.*)

PIGGIE. Do sit down, Clare, and stop climbing about over everybody. (*To* MRS. WADHURST.) You must forgive me—this is a madhouse—it's always like this—I can't think why——

CLARE (*in a whisper to* PETER, *having noticed* MR. BURNHAM). Why's that man got a roll of music, is he going to sing? (*She crosses to* PETER, *then returns to sit on the sofa.*)

MRS. WADHURST. Have you been in London for the whole season?

PIGGIE. Yes, it's been absolutely frightful, but my husband is getting leave soon, so we shall be able to pop off somewhere——

ALLY (*to* MR. WADHURST). I suppose you've never run across a chap in Burma called Beckwith ?

MR. WADHURST. No, I've never been to Burma.

ALLY. He's in rubber too, I believe—or tea—he's very amusing.

(*There is a pause.*)

MRS. WADHURST (*to* PIGGIE). We did hope you'd come and lunch with us one day—but I expect you're terribly busy——

PIGGIE. My dear, I'd worship it—— (*The telephone rings.*) Oh really, this telephone never stops for one minute—— (*Standing at the telephone.*) Hallo . . . Yes, speaking . . . Who ? . . . Mrs. Rawlingson . . . Oh, yes, yes, yes . . . (*She hands the telephone to* MRS. WADHURST.) Here—it's for you——

MRS. WADHURST (*astonished*). For me ? How very curious——

PIGGIE (*crosses* R.). Give me a cocktail, Bogey—I haven't had one at all yet and I'm exhausted——

(PETER *is up stage* C.)

MRS. WADHURST (*at the telephone*). Hallo . . . What . . . Who ? . . . I'm afraid I don't quite understand . . .

BOGEY (*giving* PIGGIE *a cocktail*). Here you are—it's a bit weak——

MRS. WADHURST (*still floundering*). . . . I think there must be some mistake . . . Just a moment . . . (*To* PIGGIE.) It's for you, Lady Maureen—a Mrs. Rawlingson——

PIGGIE (*laughing*). Now isn't that the most extraordinary coincidence—— (*She takes the telephone.*) . . . Hallo . . . Yes—speaking . . . (*She listens and her face changes.*) Oh yes . . .

(PETER *goes* L. *of the telephone table.*)

(*She looks hurriedly at the* WADHURSTS, *then at* PETER.)

I'm so awfully sorry, I only just came in . . . Oh, what a shame . . . No, no, no, it doesn't matter a bit . . . No—indeed you must call me up the first moment he gets over it . . . Yes . . . I expect it was . . . Yes . . . Good-bye.

(*She slowly hangs up the receiver, looking at the* WAD-HURSTS *in complete bewilderment. She makes a sign to* PETER *over* MRS. WADHURST'S *shoulder, but he only shakes his head.*)

(*Brightly, but with intense meaning.*) That was Mrs. Rawlingson.

PETER. Good God!

PIGGIE (*with purpose, sitting next to* MRS. WADHURST, *who is still seated on the sofa*). Did you ever meet the Rawlingsons out East?

MRS. WADHURST. No—I don't know them.

PIGGIE. Maud and I stayed with them too, you know.

MRS. WADHURST. Where?

PIGGIE. It was in Malaya somewhere, I think—I do get so muddled.

MRS. WADHURST. I think we should have heard of them if they lived in Malaya.

(PETER *meanwhile has gone to the piano and started to strum idly—he begins to hum lightly at the same time.*)

PETER (*humming to a waltz refrain, slightly indistinctly, but clearly enough for* PIGGIE *to hear*). " If these are not them, who are they? Who are they? Who are they? "

(PIGGIE *rises and saunters over to the piano.*)

PIGGIE (*up stage to* PETER). Play the other bit, dear, out of the second act—(*she hums*)—you know—" I haven't the faintest idea—oh, no—I haven't the faintest idea."

PETER (*changing tempo*). " Under the light of the moon, dear—you'd better find out pretty soon, dear."

CLARE. What on earth's that out of?

PIGGIE. Don't be silly, Clare—all I ask is that you shouldn't be *silly*! (*She moves up stage.*)

CLARE (*understanding*). Oh yes—I see.

(*There is a silence except for* PETER's *playing—everybody looks covertly at the* WADHURSTS. PIGGIE *goes over to* MR. WADHURST.)

PIGGIE (*with determination*). What ship did you come home in? (*At top of the sofa.*)

MR. WADHURST. The "Naldera."

ALLY. P. & O. ?

MRS. WADHURST. Yes.

PIGGIE. I suppose you got on at Singapore?

MR. WADHURST. No, Penang.

PIGGIE (*the light breaking*). Penang! Of course, Penang.

MRS. WADHURST. Yes, we have some friends there, so we went by train from Singapore and stayed with them for a couple of days before catching the boat.

PIGGIE (*sunk again*). Oh, yes—yes, I see.

PETER (*at the piano, humming to a march time*). "When you hear those drums rat-a-plan—rat-a-plan—find out the name of the place if you can—la la la la, la la la la——

(PIGGIE *moves down and up stage.*)

PIGGIE (*persevering*). How far is your house from the sea? Maud and I were arguing about it for hours the other day——

MR. WADHURST. It's right on the sea.

PIGGIE. That's exactly what I said, but you know Maud's so vague—she never remembers a thing——

CLARE. I suppose it's hell hot all the year round where you are?

MRS. WADHURST. Yes, the climate is a little trying, but one gets used to it.

BOGEY. Are you far from Kuala Lumpur.

MRS. WADHURST. Yes, a long way.

BOGEY. Oh, I knew some people in Kuala Lumpur once.

MR. WADHURST. What were their names ?

BOGEY. Damn it, I've forgotten—something like Harrison——

PIGGIE (*helpfully*). Morrison ?

BOGEY. No.

ALLY. Williamson ?

BOGEY. No.

PETER. Lightfoot.

BOGEY. No, it's gone——

PIGGIE (*irritably*). Never mind—it couldn't matter less really, could it ?

MRS. WADHURST (*rising*). I'm afraid we must really go now, Lady Maureen——

PIGGIE. Oh, no—please——

MRS. WADHURST. We have to dress because we're dining and going to the theatre—that's the one thing we do miss dreadfully in Pendarla—the theatre——

PIGGIE (*remembering everything—turns to* PETER, *who plays final chord*). Pendarla—— Oh dear, what a long way away it seems—— Dear Mrs. Wadhurst—(*she shoots a triumphant glance at* PETER)—it's been so lovely having this little peep at you—you and Mr. Wadhurst must come and dine quietly one night and we'll go to another theatre——

MRS. WADHURST. That would be delightful—Fred——

MR. WADHURST. Good-bye.

PIGGIE. Peter—come and say good-bye to Mr. and Mrs. Wadhurst.

PETER (*coming over* C. *and shaking hands*). Good-bye—I can never tell you how grateful I am to you for having been so kind and hospitable to my wife——

MRS. WADHURST. Next time, I hope you'll come and call on us too.

PETER. I should love to.

(CLARE *rises.*)

MRS. WADHURST. Good-bye.

CLARE. Good-bye——

(*Everybody says good-bye and shakes hands.* PETER *opens the door* R. *for the* WADHURSTS *and they go out on a wave of popularity. He goes out into the hall with them, closing the door after him.* PIGGIE *collapses on to the sofa.*)

PIGGIE (*hysterically*). Oh, my God, that was the most awful half an hour I've ever spent——

CLARE. I thought it all went down like a dinner.

PIGGIE (*rising and moving about* C.). I remember it all now; we stayed one night with them on our way from Siam—a man in Bangkok had wired to them or something—— (*She sits on the sofa.*)

ALLY. That was a nice bit you did about the old native dancing with a sword——

PIGGIE. Oh dear, they must have thought I was drunk.

(PETER *re-enters.*)

PETER. Next time you travel, my darling, I suggest you keep a diary——

PIGGIE. Wasn't it frightful—poor angels—I must ring up Maud—— (*She dials a number.*) I think they had a heavenly time though, don't you—I mean they couldn't have noticed a thing——

PETER. Oh no, the whole affair was managed with the utmost subtlety—I congratulate you——

PIGGIE. Don't be sour, Peter—— (*At the telephone.*) Hallo . . . Maud ? . . . Darling, it's not the Rawlingsons at all, it's the Wadhursts . . . (*To everybody.*) Good heavens, I never gave them Maud's address. (*At the telephone.*) . . . I forgot to give them your address . . . How can you be so unkind, Maud, you ought to be ashamed of yourself . . . They're absolute pets, both of them . . .

PETER. Come on, Ally, I've got to dress——

ALLY. All right——

CLARE. Shall I see you on Sunday ?

ALLY. Yes—I'll be over——

PIGGIE (*at the telephone*). . . . They had a lovely time and everybody was divine to them . . .

CLARE (*picking up her bag, she moves over to the piano for her gloves and hat*). Come on, Bogey, we must go too——

PIGGIE. Wait a minute, don't leave me—I've got to do my feet. (*At the telephone.*) . . . No, I was talking to Clare . . . My dear, I know, she rang me up too—she's staying with Norman . . . Phyllis will be as sour as a quince . . .

(PETER *and* ALLY *go off* L.C., *talking.*)

CLARE. Darling, I really *must* go——

PIGGIE. Wait a moment. (*At the telephone.*) . . . All right—I'll try to get hold of them in the morning and put them off. I do think it's horrid of you, though. After all, they were frightfully sweet to us . . . I've done all I can . . . Well, there's no need to get into a rage, I'm the one to get into a rage . . . Yes, you are, I can hear you. Your teeth are chattering like dice in a box . . . Oh, all right! (*She hangs up.*) Maud's impossible——

CLARE. Listen, Piggie——

PIGGIE. Wait just one minute, I've got to get the things to do my feet——

(*She rushes out of the room up* L.C.)

CLARE. I really don't see why we should all wait about—— (*She suddenly sees* MR. BURNHAM.) Oh—hallo.

MR. BURNHAM (*nervously*). Hallo. (*He rises and pushes the plans into* CLARE'S *face.*)

CLARE. I thought you'd left with your mother and father.

MR. BURNHAM. They weren't my mother and father —I'm from Freeman's. I've brought the designs for the Commander's speed-boat. Mr. Driscoll couldn't come——

CLARE. Well, you'd better wait—he'll be back soon——

MR. BURNHAM. I'm afraid I can't wait much longer —I have to get back to the shop——

CLARE.   You should have piped up before——
BOGEY.   Listen, Clare, we must push off——
CLARE.   All right.

(MR. BURNHAM *retires again into the shadows as* PIGGIE *returns with several bottles, a towel and a pair of scissors. She sits on the sofa and takes her shoes and stockings off.*)

PIGGIE.   The trouble with Maud is, she's too insular——
CLARE.   Are you driving down on Saturday?
PIGGIE.   Yes—I promised to step off at Godalming and have a cutlet with Freda on the way—do you want to come?
CLARE.   You know perfectly well I hate Freda's guts.
PIGGIE (*beginning on her feet*).   All right, darling—I'll expect you in the afternoon——

(*The telephone rings—*PIGGIE *reaches for it with one hand and goes on painting her toe-nails with the other.*)

(*At the telephone.*) Hallo . . . Yes. Oh, David, I'm *so* sorry—I completely forgot . . .

(CLARE *and* BOGEY *kiss good-bye at her. She waves to them, and they go out.*)

I couldn't help it, I had to be sweet to some people that Maud and I stayed with in Malaya . . . Oh, David darling, don't be so soured up . . . Yes, of course I do, don't be so silly . . . No, I'm quite alone doing my feet . . . Well, I can't help that, I happen to *like* them red . . . Well, after all, they are my feet; I suppose I can paint them blue if I want to . . .

(MR. BURNHAM *takes a drink and begins to tiptoe out of the room; he leaves his roll of designs on the table.* PIGGIE *catches sight of him just as he is gingerly opening the door.*)

(*To* MR. BURNHAM.) Oh, good-bye—it's been absolutely lovely, you're the sweetest family I've ever met in my life——

CURTAIN.

PROPERTY PLOT

As used at the Phœnix Theatre
(Items in italics are doubled with " The Astonished Heart ")

Large carpet covering stage.
Net curtains on rod.
Light curtains and pelmet, tie-backs.

1. *Walnut three-drawer table.* On it : glass tray, 6 bottles of gin, brandy, vermouth, etc. Sliver tub of ice and ice-tongs, syphon of soda, *decanter* of whisky, *silver salver* with 5 *cocktail glasses* and *empty shaker*, 6 large tumblers, glass dish of olives, *brass cigarette-box* with cigarettes, box of matches, *glass matchstand* and club matches, *glass ashtray.*
2. Light upholstered stool.
3. Half-round cabinet with white glass vase and lilies, magazine, glass dish of cocktail biscuits, *double ashtray*, box of matches, photo in frame of woman and child.
4. *White mantelpiece* with number of visiting and invitation cards, 3 metal photo-frames, 2 china ornaments, *small green ashtray*, small fancy box, box of matches.
5. *Steel fender and fireirons.*
6. *Round book table* with double-handled vase of mimosa, 2 French novels, *leaf ashtray*, box of matches.
7. *Upholstered armchair* in light cover.
8. Pouffe cushion.
9. *Leather couch* with light cover, 2 cushions.
10. *Open front cabinet* with 10 ornaments wired, and on top china duck.
11. Duet stool.
12. Baby grand piano with green and white vase of magnolias, photo (Peter) in silver frame, *large silver box* of cigarettes, box of matches, several pieces of music, green glass ashtray, white table mirror.
13. Small green upholstered chair.
14. *Mahogany console table* (6 legs) with white telephone, large shell, *large glass club matchstand*, box of matches, *green shell ashtray*, brown leather notebook and pencil, painted wood cigarette-box and cigarettes.
15. Green upholstered armchair (on backing R.).
Gilt frame picture of girl (on backing R.).

Roll of plans (off R.).
Hunting picture (on backing L.C.).
Mahogany chair (on backing L.C.).
Roll of cotton wool ⎫
Nail-file, nail-polish ⎬ Off stage L.C.
Small huckaback towel ⎭
Round mirror over mantelpiece.
Picture over cabinet (3).
Map down stage L.
Picture down stage R. (over 1).

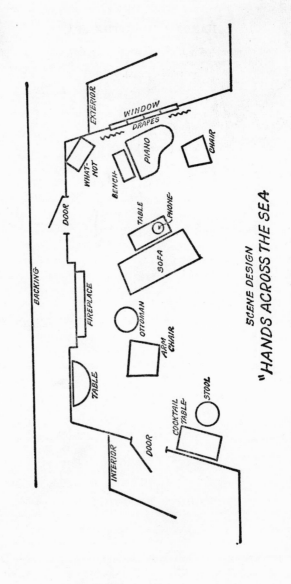

SCENE DESIGN
"HANDS ACROSS THE SEA"